Old BIRMINGHAM - The City

by
Eric Armstrong

Partly because of their mobility and hence visibility to many people, decorated trams were popular for celebratory occasions. The king and queen referred to on this one were George V and Mary. 'M R' perhaps denotes Mary Regina. A casual glance suggests that 9 is the number of the tram, but a closer look shows the sign to be a G.

© Eric Armstrong 1999
First published in the United Kingdom, 1999,
by Stenlake Publishing, Ochiltree Sawmill, The Lade,
Ochiltree, Ayrshire, KA18 2NX
Telephone / Fax: 01290 423114

ISBN 1 84033 073 2

THE PUBLISHERS REGRET THAT THEY CANNOT SUPPLY
COPIES OF ANY PICTURES FEATURED IN THIS BOOK.

FURTHER READING

The books listed below were used by the author during his research. None of them are available from Stenlake Publishing. Those interested in finding out more are advised to contact their local bookshop or reference library.

Birmingham on Old Postcards, John Marks, Vol. 1, 1990;
Reflections o...

Birmingham's ... No. 11,
Reflections o...

Birmingham ... Reflections of a Bygone Age...

Central Birmi... s, Chalford, 1995.

Birmingham A... blic Libraries in a...

Memories of a ... 1981.

Salute to Snow... 1852-1977, Derek Harris...

Growing Up an... ble from bookshops pri...

Excerpts from the author's schoolboy diaries for 1938, 1939, and 1940, when...

For many years the historic Bull Ring was the best-known area of central Birmi... xpressway and ring road it was much loved by Brummies. With its splendid market hall, ra... osphere of good-humoured hustle and bustle, the Bull Ring was a highly entertaining place... g suburbs and from beyond the boundaries of the city would come and go on Midland Re... 's Church.

Birmingham Town Hall was designed to seat 4,000 people. Although not completed until some years later, the hall was first opened to the public with a celebratory musical festival in 1834. One of the hall's architects was Joseph Hansom, designer of the hansom cab. The statue is of Sir Robert Peel, 'father' of the modern police force.

The entrance to Snow Hill station is at ground level in Colmore Row, at the centre of a building originally designed as the station hotel. The station was built on a long, narrow strip of land bounded by Snow Hill on one side, and Livery Street (where the tram stands) on the other. Anyone looking grumpy would be described by a Brummie as having 'a face as long as Livery Street'.

Snow Hill station, one of Birmingham's two main line stations, was opened in 1852 and modified and extended in 1871 and 1912. It was built to take all the Great Western Railway routes through the city. This photograph is thought to have been taken in 1918. Walls of salt-glazed bricks with buff terracotta cornices, in a style befitting this major station, can be seen behind the coaches. The first phase of Snow Hill station's history lasted for a century and a quarter (1852-1977). Passenger services, mainline and suburban, were resumed *c.*1989. A modern station building has replaced the Victorian one.

5

Postmarked 1924, this card of Colmore Row includes an interesting variety of vehicles, including a 3-wheeled car. Colmore Row runs from where the trams stand towards the camera as far as Birmingham's Council House, the seat of local government. The iron railings on the right surrounded the cathedral churchyard and were removed in the early 1940s to be converted into armaments. Before becoming Colmore Row, this thoroughfare had been given seven different names in succession, including Haymarket and Mount Pleasant.

The Cathedral, Birmingham

St Philip's Anglican Cathedral in Colmore Row is noted for its stained glass windows, designed by Sir Edward Burne-Jones (1833-1898). An eminent Victorian painter and leading member of the pre-Raphaelite movement, Burne-Jones was born in Birmingham. Important civic services are held in the Baroque-style cathedral. In the past these have included a celebration of the Coronation of George VI and Queen Elizabeth on 12 May 1937, and in 1966 the award of university status to the city's College of Advanced Technology (when it became the University of Aston). The churchyard is criss-crossed with a number of paths, providing convenient short-cuts for pedestrians.

Birmingham's Council House, an imposing example of Victorian civic pride and confidence, was built between 1874 and 1879. The foundation stone was laid by Joseph Chamberlain, arguably Birmingham's most famous citizen, the then mayor and Cabinet minister to be. The statues are of Edward VII and Queen Victoria.

The University from Chamberlain Square, Birmingham.

Chamberlain Square. The fountain, to honour Joseph Chamberlain, was inaugurated in 1880. Behind the seated statue of Sir Josiah Mason, industrialist and philanthropist, is Mason's College, opened in 1880 and granted university status in 1900. It formed the nucleus of Birmingham University. The rounded corner to the left was part of the city's principal public library. *14 June 1940. Went up to University, Edmund St . . . with John & Syd for Oral Examination in French . . . hoping for the best.* (Schooldays almost at an end.) The Norwich Union building, right, had earlier housed the Liberal Club.

A postcard of the library and reading room postmarked 20 December 1905. This spacious high-domed reference library served as a second home to thousands of students over many years. Efficient and courteous though they were, library assistants could not help but make some clatter as they darted around the gallery! The library remained in service until 1974.

FREE PUBLIC LIBRARY, RATCLIFF PLACE, BIRMINGHAM.   212776 J.V.

The statue is of James Watt (1736-1819), whose work on steam engines in Birmingham gave great impetus to the Industrial Revolution. The town hall is on the right, while in the background on the left part of Mason's College (the city centre part of the University in days past) is visible. This housed the Arts Faculty when the author was a student (1947-1950). The rounded building on the left was known as the Midland Institute, the library in the previous picture being an extension of the Institute which was built in 1857 and demolished in 1965.

The Hall of Memory, built to honour the fallen of the First World War. Situated a short distance to the west of the town hall, it became part of an expanded civic centre area along with its adjacent garden. A 'grand design' was prepared to redevelop this part of the city after World War I, including a projected 9 acre underground car park for 1,200 cars, although few of the ambitious plans were realised before the end of World War II. Broad Street can just be seen on the left of the picture.

MUNICIPAL BANK AND MASONIC HALL, BIRMINGHAM.

Imposing new buildings roughly opposite the Hall of Memory on the south side of Broad Street. The Birmingham Municipal Bank stands to the right, with the Masonic Hall on its left. The bank later became a branch of the TSB, and when the masons moved to other premises the Masonic Hall was used as offices by a broadcasting company. Both buildings were designed to harmonise with those envisaged for the planned civic centre.

GENERAL POST OFFICE, BIRMINGHAM.

Birmingham's main post office (designed by Sir H. Tanner), standing solidly between the top of Pinfold Street (left) and Hill Street (right). Opened to the public in 1890, this post office was held in great affection by many Brummies. When threatened with demolition after the Second World War, public opinion was instrumental in ensuring that the building survived. It still stands, although only limited use is made of it by the post office now. The higher signposts point to Kidderminster and Wolverhampton and the lower ones to Bromsgrove, Worcester and Redditch.

New Street, one of Birmingham's busiest shopping streets, lending credence to Napoleon's alleged jibe that Britain is 'a nation of shopkeepers'. The building on the extreme right housed the offices of the Birmingham Post and Mail newspapers. The postcard was sent in May 1939.

Postmarked 1927, this view looks westwards along New Street towards the town hall. In the foreground, to the left of the open-top bus, Stephenson Place leads to New Street station. To the right of the white-coated policeman is the beginning (city centre end) of Corporation Street. A branch of Barclays Bank is just discernible in the left foreground.

16

Designed by Sir Charles Barry (architect of the Palace of Westminster), King Edward's Grammar School, Birmingham's premier grammar school, was built in 1833 in the eastern section of New Street. The building was demolished in 1936 and the school moved to a brand new building on the Bristol Road, Edgbaston.

The plush interior of W. J. Greatrex's 'Gentlemen's Hairdressing Establishment' at 111 New Street. An undoubted cut above the 'short back and sides' barbers!

The Waterloo Bar, G. W. HARDY, PROPRIETOR.

New Street, BIRMINGHAM.

FREE HOUSE. TELEPHONE 04550.

A companion postcard of the interior of the Waterloo Bar, dating from about 1912, displays solid, elegant wooden fixtures and fittings, spotless table-cloths and snowy napkins. At the time, billiards was far more popular than snooker.

A pigeon's eye view across Stephenson Place, near New Street station, towards the beginning of Corporation Street. Initially some seven acres of slums were cleared to make way for the station, on which work began in 1846. The railed areas in the foreground shield the steps leading to the underground public conveniences which meant 'spending a penny' for ladies, but were gratis for men.

26 December 1940. Met Eddie and went to Snack bar opp. New St. Stn. 'The High Hat'. Had Egg & Chips, bread and butter, biscuits and coffee. Quite a decent little place. (17-year-old 'sophisticates' out on the town on Boxing Day.)

19

New Street Station, Birmingham.

New Street station, the main LMS Railway station in Birmingham. Dating from the 1850s, the station was doubled in size to straddle Queens Drive in 1880. It was covered by a massive iron and glass roof, thought at the time to be the largest single-span roof in the world, being some 370 yards long, 70 yards wide, and 27 yards high. Platforms were connected both by a bridge and subways. The original station took seven years to build and cost £500,000. The Stephensons, father George and son Robert, were the appointed engineers for the building of the London and Birmingham Railway during the 1830s.

CORPORATION STREET, BIRMINGHAM.

Corporation Street, the longest city centre street, thronged with shoppers. The building of this street owes much to the drive and vision of Joseph Chamberlain, who used enabling legislation to clear away some of the city's worst slums in order for work to begin on it in 1878. By the time this picture was taken some attempt was being made to regulate traffic with traffic lights. The bus is making for Quinton, one of the newer, outer suburbs to the west of the city centre. The high, slender tower of Central Hall can be seen in the distance.

Corporation Street photographed from Cherry Street. Postmarked 1928, the picture shows the spiked helmet that was still worn by policemen at the time. The premises of the Midland Educational bookshop, a fine, well-patronised shop which specialised in school books, stand immediately to the left of the KODAK sign.

The entrance to the North Western Arcade, an extension of the Great Western Arcade (built above the tunnel into Snow Hill station) is on the left, on the near side of the junction with Bull Street. Lewis's ('over 200 shops in one'), one of the major city-centre department stores, stands further down the street and contrasts sharply with the kerbside 'merchants' in the middle distance.

Lewis's in its 1930s splendour, with all flags flying. On Wednesday 2 September 1931 those with a bob or two could have listened to Jan Berenska and the Lewis's orchestra playing a 'Musical Comedy Switch' as they ate a three-course table d'hote luncheon for 1/9 or a five-course one for half-a-crown. Between 10 and 11.30 a.m., 'Coffee, with Cream, and Biscuit or Cigarette' could be enjoyed for 3d; a linen serviette cost 1 penny extra.

Corporation Street, Birmingham

Once past Bull Street, (lower) Corporation Street contained fewer shops but some fine public buildings. From the clothes and vehicles on view, this is probably a pre-World War I card. At the time anybody who was anybody boasted a piano in the parlour, and many middle class children had to endure piano lessons, whether they were musically gifted or not.

LAW COURTS, BIRMINGHAM.

Queen Victoria laid the foundation stone of this suitably magisterial building, situated in lower Corporation Street. The courts housed in it are still busily in session, but have since been supplemented by what are colloquially known as the 'QE II courts'.

Situated almost opposite the law courts, this splendid redbrick structure housed the 'HQ' (in Birmingham) of the Methodist Church. This card of the Central Hall was posted in 1931, its message reading, ' ...the Ordination is on Tuesday. I have got good digs. Preaching at Tipton on Sunday.' Tipton lies in the heart of the Black Country, a little to the north and east of Dudley.

The hall was used for lay as well as religious purposes. *23 November 1938. Speech Day . . . Central Hall. I took tickets at top of stairs. Margaret came with* (her) *Mom. Had prize.* At the time I was a 15-year-old junior prefect from Handsworth Grammar School, highly excited what with responsibility, romance and recognition.

27

NEW FIRE STATION, BIRMINGHAM.

Birmingham's state-of-the-art central fire station, photographed when new in the 1930s. Situated at the end of lower Corporation Street overlooking Lancaster Place, the station was well placed to tackle fires in the city centre during Birmingham's blitz of 1940-1941.

General Hospital, Birmingham

For a time, this was Birmingham's finest hospital. Situated in Steelhouse Lane, it received its first patients in 1897. 340 beds were available. All too soon, the cheery red bricks became soot begrimed in the city's industrial atmosphere. The hospital was opened by Princess Christian, daughter of Queen Victoria, and replaced an earlier general hospital which had been opened in 1779.

The Wesleyan and General Insurance Company's offices and clock, along with the tram stops for trams to Erdington (No. 2), Stockland Green and Short Heath, were located in Steelhouse Lane. In the middle-distance, a car is turning left out of Bull Street into Colmore Row, where, at the far end, some of the columns of the town hall can be seen.

Bull Street was another favourite thoroughfare for a shopping spree and home to Grey's, a major department store not far from its rival, Lewis's. 'Go all over town and then find it at Grey's' was a well-known saying. 93 Bull Street is an address of historic importance, for the shop located there formed the beginnings of what became the Cadbury cocoa and chocolate industrial empire.

Inset: George Cadbury (1839-1922) and his brother Richard expanded their father's business to establish a 'factory in a garden' in Bournville. As Quakers, the Cadbury family took a keen interest in social conditions, introducing enlightened employment practices, plus socially advanced housing in their model village.

The message on this postcard of the High Street reads: 'This is a side street in the business part of Brummagem. The opening on the left leads into a big arcade.' The Turkish Baths seem well located to cope with weary (male only?) shoppers and businessmen. High Street ran from Bull Street.

The splendid interior of Birmingham's principal Congregational Church. Writing in 1907, the card's sender commented, '... on Sunday morning we were sitting upstairs on the left hand side, it was so nice, and the singing was grand.' *20 November 1938. Went to Carr's Lane in afternoon. Congregational Rally. Walked from town.* (Back home to Handsworth - 3 or 4 miles distant.) Carr's Lane is a side street off High Street.

33

This postcard of the High Street, sent to Dresden on 18 October 1929 and addressed to the director of a publishing firm, carries a long message in German, written in tiny writing. The writer tells of his stormy crossing and is proud that he was not sea sick. With his Baedeker guide book, he plans to visit Birmingham churches and the museum. If the German visitor had walked in the direction in which the first car is facing, he would soon have been in the Bull Ring. On the left, High Street curves into New Street at its eastern end.

Great Western Arcade, Birmingham.

Birmingham was fortunate in having a number of attractive shopping arcades including Great Western, North Western, City and Midland Arcades. The Great Western Arcade, the first to be built in the city (1875-1876) followed the line of the Great Western railway tunnel.

City Arcade, Birmingham.

The arcades provided splendid places for window shopping, sheltering from the rain, taking safe short cuts between one busy street and another, or just whiling away the odd half hour.

The historic Bull Ring was once the site of Birmingham's village green. The right to hold markets there was granted more than 800 years ago. Barrows, stalls, orators, entertainers, a large indoor market and jostling, good-natured crowds all combined to create what was for many Brummies the best feature of the city centre, and one that was held in great affection. The church is St Martin's. In the foreground, right, a poster for the Grand Theatre gives Mrs (Lily) Langtry ('The Jersey Lily') top billing.

This card shows the rear entrance of the Market Hall in Worcester Street (the front entrance is illustrated on the cover). The hall, which was opened in 1835, was 365 feet long, 108 feet wide and 60 feet high with four main avenues. The lad on the bike has a container of some sort hanging from one handlebar and is probably an errand boy.

Traders in the Market Hall preparing to serve hungry and thirsty shoppers. In the 1930s pork sandwiches (priced 3d), and bread soaked in dripping (1d) were popular. Dripping formed part of the staple diet in many homes between the wars.

26 August 1940. Market Hall has been burned to ground, only skeleton remaining. Delayed action bombs in Perry Barr, back of Odeon . . .

The earliest St Martin's church to stand on this site was built during the eleventh century. It was subsequently rebuilt several times, and the church shown here, designed in the Gothic style, was consecrated in 1875. Just visible is a row of shelters for passengers waiting for Midland Red buses. A crowd has also gathered - possibly to listen to a soapbox orator. *11 April 1938. Elijah presented by School Choir at St Martins Church, Bull Ring. Singing OK. But music rotten except for a few* (bits). *Music critic, aged 15 - just.*

A different aspect of the Bull Ring, and wholesale as distinct from retail.

41

Old House at Deritend, Birmingham

Most of the Old Crown Inn is thought to date from the sixteenth century, and is of particular interest because of the rarity of half-timbered buildings in an industrial city. Post World War II road widening left the inn unscathed and with city authority help it has recently been restored.

A royal visit on 7 July 1909 for the opening of the new redbrick Birmingham University building on the Bristol Road, Edgbaston. Queen Alexandra is already seated in the horse-drawn carriage, and the top hatted King Edward VII is just about to sit down beside her. Soldiers at the slope arms position can just be seen on the platform of New Street station.

A number of Birmingham trade organisations erected triumphal arches along the route of the royal visit of 1909. Brass bedsteads were made in their thousands in Birmingham and this arch, in Temple Row, reads, 'Loyal Greetings From The Metallic Bedstead Manufacturers'.

The face that launched - not a thousand ships - but thousands of post and cigarette cards bearing its image. Gladys Cooper (1888-1971) was a popular beauty and actress who was awarded the DBE in 1967. This publicity card was issued by the Scala Theatre, Smallbrook Street, Birmingham where Gladys was billed as 'A Scala Favourite for February'.

Under the inspired and inspiring leadership of Sir Barry Jackson (1879-1961), Birmingham Repertory Theatre became a leading provincial theatre between the two World Wars. No prizes for identifying the king on the card! Sir Barry also founded the Malvern (Arts) Festival.

A postcard of the Birmingham Co-operative Society's Jubilee Exhibition of 1931 in the Bingley Hall, celebrating 50 years of the society. The co-op played a central role in the lives of many Brummies, especially working class ones. The dividend ('divvy') it paid to its customers provided many hard-up mothers with the means to keep their children looking respectable.

This 'pulling together' postcard was sent in November 1944 and bears the printed message: 'This is a time for everyone to stand together, and hold firm! - the Prime Minister', as well as stating that the cost of the picture was borne by Messrs. LINREAD, Ltd., Bolt Screw and Rivet Manufacturers... Birmingham'. The sender of the card has written 'You can see I am putting all my money into war savings'.

Although born and educated in London, Joseph Chamberlain (affectionately known as Joe) first made his political mark in Birmingham. Born in 1836, he joined the Birmingham screw manufacturing firm of Nettlefolds in the 1850s, where he made his fortune. Chamberlain entered public life in 1868 as a Birmingham town councillor, and served as mayor from 1873 to 1876 (he retired from Nettlefolds in 1874).

He had a reputation for radicalism, and earned the nickname of 'the gas and water socialist' because of his work to take the city's gas and water supply into municipal ownership. He also worked hard and effectively to improve Birmingham's housing stock, assisted by an Act of 1875 which allowed local councils to clear away slums and introduce schemes of urban redevelopment. Chamberlain's drive and vision made sure that Birmingham was in the forefront of such changes in England, with Glasgow taking the lead in Scotland. In 1876 Chamberlain was elected, unopposed, to Parliament as an MP for Birmingham. After serving as President of the Board of Trade he became, in 1895, an enlightened, imaginative and efficient Secretary for the Colonies. He also became the first Chancellor of Birmingham University, whose interests he did much to promote.